BEACHSIDE BOHEMIAN

MENTO

Atlântico

Estrada de Asfalto
Estrada de Terra
Calçamento

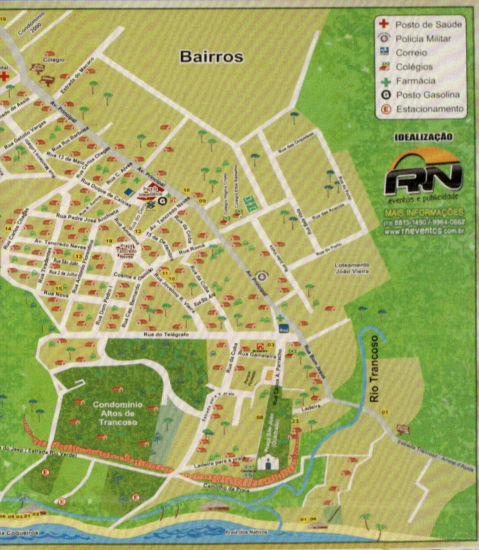

Bairros

Condomínio 2000

Colégio

Rio Trancoso

Condomínio
Altos de
Trancoso

Loteamento
João Vieira

Praia dos Nativos

+ Posto de Saúde
▣ Polícia Militar
▣ Correio
▣ Colégios
+ Farmácia
G Posto Gasolina
E Estacionamento

IDEALIZAÇÃO

RN
eventos e publicidade

MAIS INFORMAÇÕES
(73) 8813-1490 / 9964-0662
www.rneventos.com.br

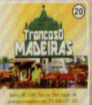

A DESIGNER COUPLE'S REFUGE FOR FAMILY AND FRIENDS

BEACHSIDE BOHEMIAN

EASY LIVING BY THE SEA

ROBERT AND CORTNEY NOVOGRATZ

WITH MICHELLE BILLODEAU

RIZZOLI
NEW YORK

New York · Paris · London · Milan

CONTENTS

PREFACE

We wrote this book to share one of the best things we've ever done for our family—buying a home in Trancoso, Brazil. When Robert and I visited over ten years ago, we fell in love with everything about it—the warm ocean, the wildlife and plants, and the food, culture, and music. But most of all, we fell in love with the people. Brazil is a culture driven by seemingly contradictory influences: a strong connection to religion and a deep indulgence in sensual pleasures—good food and drink, and of course sex, which is an interesting mix as you can imagine. We have always been risk takers—we started our design business by building and rehabbing houses in New York City while raising seven kids—but buying property in Trancoso was the biggest risk we've ever taken. We didn't speak a word of Portuguese then, but we managed to communicate well enough, and the locals embraced us with open arms. We've been to so many extraordinary countries that are equally as artistic and beautiful, but Brazil's love for children is unmatched. When we realized that our kids weren't being shushed at every turn, we knew we had found a very special place. In our wildest dreams, we never thought we'd own a home in such an exotic and awe-inspiring place.

We took a leap into the unknown and have learned a lot. We've been able to really immerse ourselves in a different culture. There's no doubt that the way Brazilians approach life is very similar to ours—they want to truly enjoy it in every way possible, so that felt familiar. But living—even for short stints—in a new place means that you have to change your habits and switch things up. In addition to being able to appreciate nature in a whole new way, the ability to alter our routine and dig into new experiences has been hugely valuable, not just for me and Robert, but certainly for our kids as well.

The home has also had a practical upside: we've been able to contribute to our family's finances by renting the house to family, friends, and even strangers. The process has allowed us to not only pay for the house's upkeep, but also to share Trancoso's beauty. In this book, we've offered tips for designing and decorating a home like a boutique hotel, so that your home always feels like a vacation destination, whether you're living your daily life there or allowing someone a glimpse of your life while you're out and about exploring other places.

We hope you learn a little bit about Trancoso, and along the way enjoy the crazy travel stories we've lived. In the end, what we really hope is that the book inspires your own adventures, and encourages you to travel outside your comfort zone. Life is one big, chaotic, and insane enterprise with the Novogratz clan, and we wouldn't want it any other way. If you ever have the opportunity to visit Trancoso, do it. There's no place like it.

—*Cortney Novogratz*

WHY TRANCOSO?

We first learned about Trancoso over ten years ago. Robert was training for a marathon and had a favorite bar near our house in SoHo called Café Noir, where he and his running buddies would grab a beer after training. (I like to think Café Noir was the real reason they all trained so diligently.) Robert eventually became friends with one of the "regulars" there—a colorful Russian architect named Alexander who was known for telling tall tales, as most bar flies are. After some time, Alexander told Robert that he had a house in Trancoso that he was putting on the market. Robert was skeptical at first, but Alexander convinced us to visit, and we instantly fell in love with the town. The property needed quite a bit of work, which we were actually thrilled about—we love investing in places that need a little TLC. More importantly, we knew what a treasure a place like Trancoso would be for our family through the years. Our lawyer told us we were crazy; we were buying a home in Brazil from a Russian who likes his spirits. But we were sold, and soon after, so was Alexander's place. Since then, we've been renovating, designing, and changing the house every time we visit.

GETTING TO KNOW TRANCOSO

Trancoso is an idyllic, unspoiled fishing village on the coast of Brazil, known by travelers and locals alike for its exotic wildlife, lush greenery, tropical weather, and warm South Atlantic Ocean waters. The town is located in the State of Bahia, the home of famed musician João Gilberto, father of the Bossa Nova rhythm. Trancoso is considered one of the earliest settlements of Jesuits in the world; it was settled shortly after the European discovery of Brazil in the 1500s. The Jesuits built one of Brazil's oldest and most beautiful churches, St. John the Baptist, around 1586. This served as the focal point for what became the town square, or Praça de São João Batista (the Square of St. John the Baptist), lined by houses, shops, restaurants, and hundred year old trees. Today, this area is known as the Quadrado, and kids and adults alike play soccer in its center field (for more on life in the Quadrado see pg. 165).

The history of the area of Bahia is rich. It's a melting pot of cultures: indigenous, Portuguese, and African. When European settlers arrived to the area in the early 1500s, they engaged in a slave trade to help grow the local economy. Between the 1520s and the 1850s, approximately 1.2 million slaves were transported to the State of Bahia from various parts of Africa. During the early nineteenth century, numerous slave revolts culminated in the largest urban slave rebellion in the history of the Americas, the Malês Revolt of 1835. Domestic and international pressures following that revolt eventually resulted in the emancipation decree of 1888 (from *Slavery to Freedom in Brazil*). As a result, Brazil's culture is deeply influenced by various African cultures. The martial art of capoeira, African derived music such as samba, and cuisine with spices and flavors native to Africa, all became an integral part of Brazilian culture.

Beginning in the 1970s, Trancoso saw a steep influx of travelers and people curious about the area. It became a refuge for people seeking tranquil surroundings and unspoiled nature. Houses resembling those in the Quadrado began popping up in the areas nearby the heart of Trancoso. In the last five years, tourism in Trancoso has skyrocketed. The fashion and design crowds have always had a big presence there, with direct flights from Milan to nearby Porto Seguro. And even though it's a getaway for the Missoni family, Anderson Cooper, Cristiano Ronaldo, Matthew McConaughey, and supermodels Kate Moss and Naomi Campbell, it's been able to retain the same charm and simplicity that we were instantly drawn to when we first traveled there. It's special being one of the few American families that frequents Trancoso, and we love when a local asks our kids if they speak Portuguese, Spanish, or French before a word of English is spoken.

WHAT A TRIP: GETTING THERE

Robert came from a large military family, so vacations to exotic places were never something he was accustomed to. In fact, he had only been on a plane once before he turned 23. He remembers getting dressed up for the flight and getting a pair of wings from the pilot. The ability to be on the other side of the country in five or six hours and on another continent in just an hour was incredibly special; no one complained if the plane was 15 minutes late. We've tried to instill a sense of appreciation in our kids that traveling to amazing places really is a privilege.

People always ask us how we fly with so many kids, and we'll say this: we've made friends and we've made enemies, but with luck and a sense of humor, we've been able to turn those adversaries into allies! I remember one flight in particular. We were all boarding the plane, kids bickering over where they were sitting of course, and Breaker had already started eating the food I'd packed. He saw Wolfie coming down the aisle of the plane and threw his half eaten sandwich at him but missed, and it hit a lady seated nearby. Robert and I were mortified. The woman froze, chuckled, and threw the sandwich right back at him. Breaker couldn't have thrown it at a cooler passenger. So much of enjoying travel is learning to have a go-with-the-flow attitude. I don't care if I sit at the back of the plane with babies on my lap, as long as I get to see the world.

TAM Airlines and American Airlines are the two airlines we use to get to Trancoso. Most flights go through São Paolo, the largest city in Brazil, and connect in Porto Seguro, a fishing village nearby Trancoso. When we land in Porto Seguro, we're greeted by one of our favorite parts of Brazil—our house manager and dear friend Paula. She's got a smile on her face, a bounce in her step, and a cooler full of beer, water, and Guaraná, our favorite Brazilian soda. The tropical humidity envelops us like a steam room, and the real journey begins. All nine of us (Robert, me, and our kids Wolfie, Tallulah, Bellamy, Breaker, Five, Holleder, and Major) climb into our VW Kombi van and set out on the hour-long drive to our house. What's truly amazing is the transition from the airplane landing strip, to paved roads, to cobblestone roads, to a ferry, and finally, to dirt roads. It's very apparent that we've stepped out of the plane into a different way of life.

The ferry near Trancoso, one of the last legs of the long journey to our house.

TRAVEL TIPS FROM CORTNEY

1. GET YOUR PASSPORT AND VISA IN ORDER WELL AHEAD OF TIME—AT LEAST 90 DAYS BEFORE YOUR TRIP.*

2. TO GET TO BRAZIL, TAKE A NIGHT FLIGHT FROM NEW YORK OR MIAMI

3. MAKE YOUR LAYOVERS LONG ENOUGH SO YOU AREN'T STRESSED WHEN CATCHING THE CONNECTING FLIGHTS, BUT NEVER MORE THAN 3 HOURS

4. DRESS IN LAYERS, AND WEAR BLACK SO MESSES DON'T SHOW

5. BRING DISPOSABLE MINI-TRAVELING TOOTHBRUSHES

6. WHEN TRAVELING WITH KIDS, BRING MAD LIBS, AN IPAD, & COLORING SUPPLIES

7. GET YOUR KIDS TO BRING THEIR OWN CARRY-ONS; IT TEACHES THEM RESPONSIBILITY

8. BRING A RECHARGEABLE BACKUP BATTERY FOR YOUR PHONE

9. GIVE THE KIDS ONE GLASS OF WINE, NEVER TWO ;))))

10. DRINKS LOTS AND LOTS OF WATER TO STAY HYDRATED—AIRPLANES HAVE VERY DRY AIR—AND TREAT YOURSELVES TO A NICE MEAL

11. BRING HAND WIPES—YOU CAN NEVER HAVE ENOUGH!

12. SNACKS LIKE ALMONDS AND PEANUTS ARE HEALTHY AND NOT TOO MESSY

13. TRAVEL LIGHT

14. DON'T FORGET YOUR SENSE OF HUMOR

* *IF YOU'RE EVER STRESSED ABOUT CARRYING PASSPORTS, THINK OF ME CARRYING 9 (YES, INCLUDING ROBERT'S AS HE TENDS TO LOSE THINGS). I'VE TEMPORARILY LOST A KID HERE AND THERE OVER THE YEARS, BUT SOMEHOW I HAVEN'T LOST A PASSPORT YET.*

WHAT TO PACK

- AS MANY SWIMSUITS AS YOU OWN

- HAVAIANAS, THE BEST FLIPS FLOPS (ALTHOUGH YOU'LL BUY SOME WHEN YOU'RE THERE)

- A BOOK OF SIMPLE PHRASES IN PORTUGUESE

- A CAMERA

- AN EXTRA DUFFLE OR OVERNIGHT BAG ROLLED UP IN YOUR SUITCASE, SO YOU CAN CARRY YOUR TRIP TREATS HOME EASILY

WHAT NOT TO PACK

- HIGH HEELS—SOME BRAZILIAN WOMEN CAN PULL THEM OFF WHILE WALKING ON THE SAND, BUT THIS AMERICAN GIRL SURE CAN'T

- A HEAVY COAT

- A BERET—BERETS ARE GREAT, BUT ON A DIFFERENT CONTINENT

- ENOUGH JEWELRY TO SINK A FERRY

CHAPTER 1

THE ARRIVAL

After the long journey and a catch-up session with Paula our house manager, we're ready to kick back and relax. If you're one of our guests, the first thing we recommend is taking off your plane shoes and donning a pair of Havaianas. Grab a cold drink of your choice and get ready for a tour from Paula and a wonderful, life-changing stay.

The house always has guests—whether they're our friends and family or someone renting it—so we like to be sure that we provide everything guests need to chill out and get comfortable. You know what it's like to travel somewhere and to realize halfway there that you've forgotten something essential? In coming up with the list of items we have for our guests (see pg. 42), we try to anticipate that inevitable moment.

THINGS WE KEEP AROUND FOR OUR GUESTS

- NOTEBOOKS FOR LEISURELY WRITING

- SUNSCREEN IN ALL DEGREES OF SPF

- SUNGLASSES & HATS

- A POLAROID CAMERA

- MAGAZINES FOR ALL AGES

- TOYS FOR THE LITTLE ONES

- ADAPTER KITS

- A TOTE FOR THE BEACH

- THE ESSENTIAL BEACH READS

- A PAIR OF BINOCULARS FOR KEEPING WATCH ON THE WILDLIFE IN THE BACKYARD

- BUG SPRAY & CITRONELLA CANDLES

- TOILETRIES IN THE BATHROOM, LIKE TOOTHPASTE, A TOOTHBRUSH, COTTON BALLS, ETC

For us, vacation is the time to connect with our family and friends free from modern distractions. We're all about hanging out with people, which is probably obvious since we have seven kids. We feel that a house with an open floor plan (see the house's floor plan on the following page) and inviting common areas really facilitates not just occupying the same space with others but really engaging with them. We were lucky that this house had an open floor plan when we bought it. We kept the layout as-is, and made the house as comfortable and inviting as a home can be. We also focused on bringing the outdoors in—we wanted to make sure nature was the focal point of every room. We think the result is a home that feels like the getaway we've always wanted and that we love sharing with others.

43

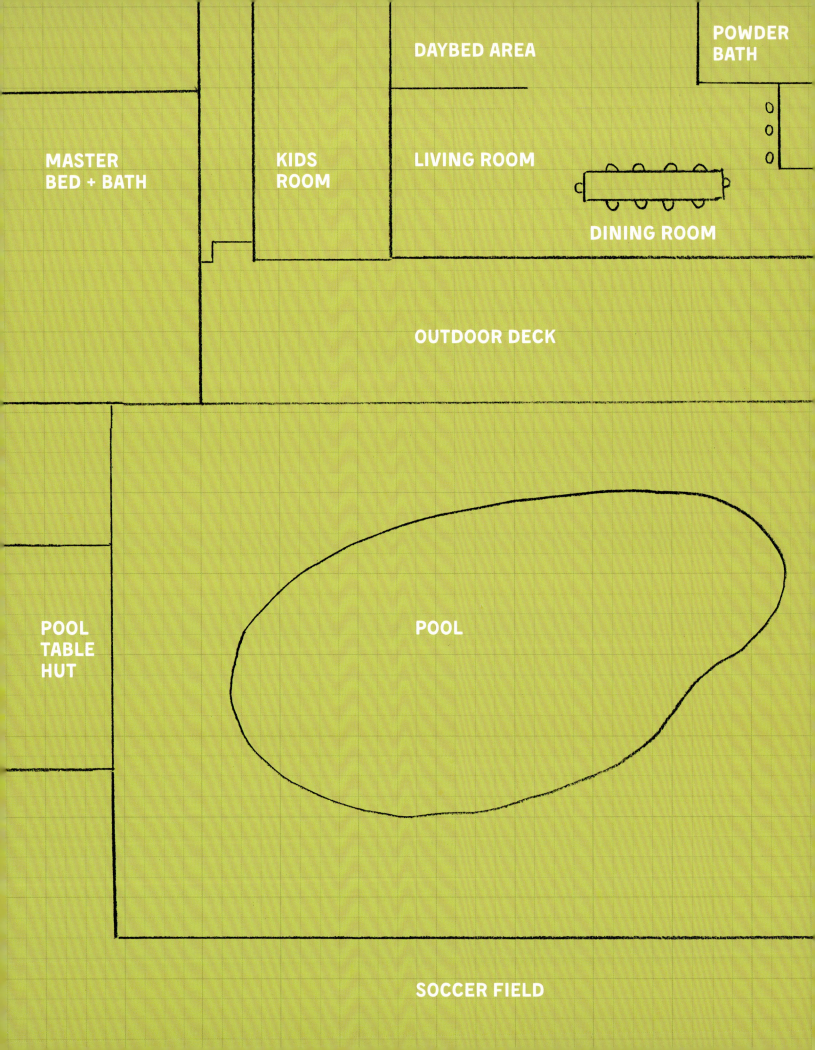

POWDER
BATH

DAYBED AREA

MASTER
BED + BATH

KIDS
ROOM

LIVING ROOM

DINING ROOM

OUTDOOR DECK

POOL
TABLE
HUT

POOL

SOCCER FIELD

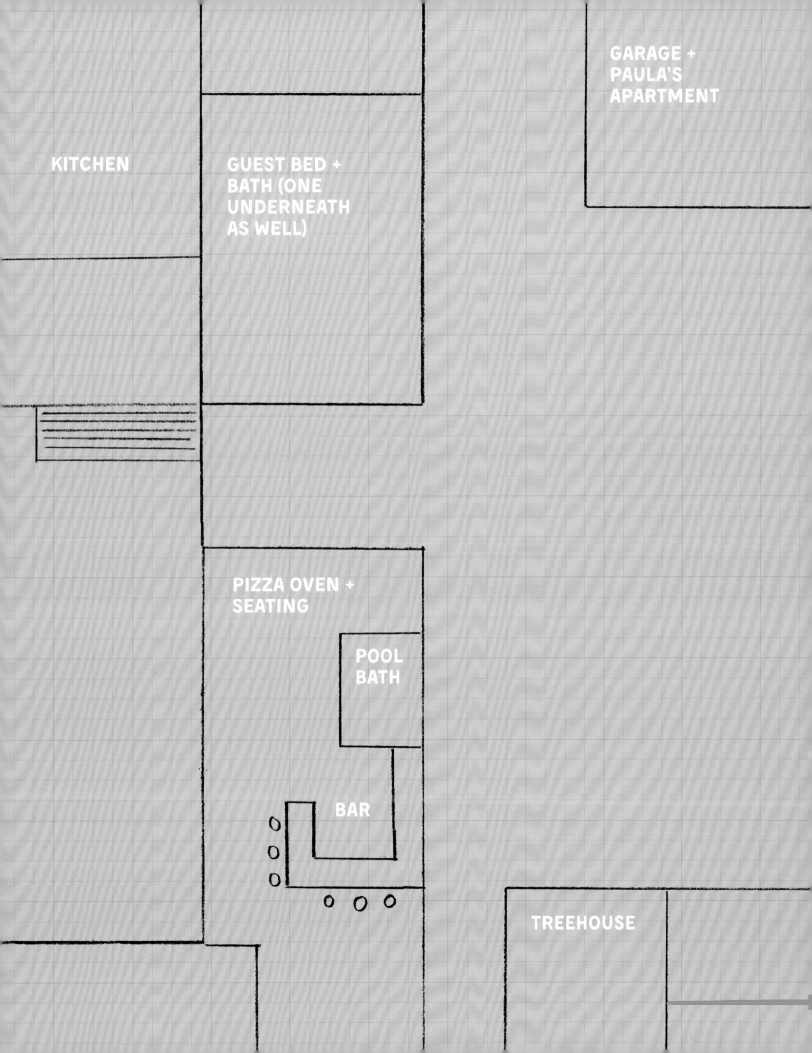

KITCHEN

GUEST BED + BATH (ONE UNDERNEATH AS WELL)

GARAGE + PAULA'S APARTMENT

PIZZA OVEN + SEATING

POOL BATH

BAR

TREEHOUSE

CHAPTER 2

THE KITCHEN

Our kitchen is a working kitchen. Whether guests prefer to entrust the cooking to our wonderful chef, or whether they would rather try their hand at a few Brazilian recipes (see pgs. 54–59 for our favorites), the kitchen is always bustling (and *never* as clean as the photographs here). We love learning about Brazilian cuisine, and we also love teaching the Brazilians a thing or two about American food. The fresh desserts made daily by the chef are unbelievably good, and nothing beats a nourishing morning spread after a late night spent dancing and keeping up with the locals. As is true of any house, the kitchen is one of the liveliest rooms.

Even if your guests plan to go out for every meal, one should still stock the kitchen with a few essentials, so that your guests have the freedom to improvise in the kitchen if the mood strikes them. The goal is to make guests feel at home, so provide them with the basics so they feel like they're in their own kitchen.

FRIDGE ESSENTIALS

- BEER & WINE

- BOTTLED WATER

- DIJON MUSTARD

- PARSLEY

- SODA

- DAIRY PRODUCTS:
  MILK, EGGS, ETC.

- FRESH FRUIT

- PIZZA INGREDIENTS

- CHOCOLATE

HOW TO MAKE A CAIPIRINHA

1 lime
1 tablespoon of fine sugar
2 ounces of cachaça (a Brazilian white rum made from sugar cane)
Crushed ice

Cut the lime in quarters then cut them
crosswise. Put lime and sugar in a tall glass
and mash with a muddler. Add the cachaça and
stir. Add ice to fill the glass and stir again.

BOLO DE FUBA
CORNMEAL CAKE

2 cups finely ground cornmeal
1 cup all purpose flour
1 1/2 cups sugar
1 tablespoon baking powder
1 cup corn oil
1/2 cup milk
1 cup buttermilk
3 eggs
1 teaspoon salt
Powdered sugar

Preheat the oven to 350 degrees. Grease a Bundt pan or angel food cake pan lightly with butter or vegetable oil. Place all of the ingredients except for the powdered sugar in a blender. Blend until well mixed. Pour mixture into prepared pan. Place cake pan in the oven and bake for 35–45 minutes, or until cake has risen and the middle of the cake springs back to the touch.

Remove cake from oven and let cool in the pan for 5–10 minutes. Loosen cake from the sides of the pan with a knife, then invert the cake onto a plate. Place the cake right side up, and dust with powdered sugar before serving.

BRIGADIERO

1 (14 ounce) can sweetened condensed milk
1 tablespoon butter
1 tablespoon cocoa
Chocolate sprinkles, shredded coconut,
  roughly chopped pistachios

Over medium-low heat, stir vigorously the first three ingredients. Cook the mixture until it thickens enough to show the pan bottom during stirring (it will be firm enough to stay together and not spread). Pour into a greased dish and let cool to room temperature (or chill a few minutes in the fridge). Grease your hands with butter and take small amounts of candy and form into 1 1/2 inch balls. Roll the balls in chocolate sprinkles, coconut, and pistachios to decorate. If the balls don't hold their shape, cook an additional 5 minutes until it thickens up more.

MOQUECA

2 1/2 pounds halibut, cut into 2 inch pieces
1 cup roughly chopped onion, plus 1 cup
  julienned onion
2 cups roughly chopped tomatoes, plus 2
  tomatoes sliced into 1/4 inch rounds
2 cloves garlic, plus 1 tablespoon minced garlic
5 tablespoons chopped fresh cilantro leaves
(continued on next page)

2 teaspoons salt
3 tablespoons fresh-squeezed lime juice
1/4 cup olive oil
1/4 cup Piri Piri (recipe follows)
1 (14.5-ounce) can coconut milk

Place the fish in a large non-reactive mixing bowl. In the carafe of a blender, combine the chopped onion, the chopped tomatoes, 2 cloves of garlic, 1 tablespoon of cilantro, 1 teaspoon of salt, and the lime juice. Blend until smooth in the blender, then pour directly over the fish. Cover with plastic wrap and refrigerate for 1 hour.

Heat a large sauté pan over medium-high heat. Add the olive oil to the pan, and once hot, add the julienned onions to the pan and sauté, stirring often until translucent, about 3–4 minutes. Add the minced garlic to the pan and sauté for an additional 30 seconds. Pour the fish and the marinade into the sauté pan and add the remaining teaspoon of salt, the Piri Piri, and the coconut milk and stir to combine. Once the liquid comes to a boil, dot the top of the pan with the sliced tomatoes and cover with a lid. Reduce the heat to medium-low and continue to cook until the flesh starts to flake, about 10 minutes.

Remove the cover from the pan and sprinkle the remaining 4 tablespoons of cilantro over the fish. Serve accompanied by steamed white rice.

PIRI PIRI

1 tablespoon, plus 1/2 cup olive oil
5 cloves garlic, smashed
1/4 cup fresh squeezed lemon juice
1/2 teaspoon salt
Cooked rice, to serve
4 cayenne chile peppers, stemmed, ribs and seeds removed,
   and rough chopped (or substitute other hot red peppers)

Heat a small sauté pan over medium-high heat. Add 1
tablespoon of the olive oil to the pan. Once the oil is
hot, add the garlic and peppers to the pan. Sauté, stirring
often, until the edges of the garlic start to turn brown,
3 to 4 minutes. Add the lemon juice to the pan, and
remove from the heat.

Place the contents of the sauté pan in a blender and
add the salt. Puree the peppers and garlic in the blender
until mostly smooth. Drizzle the remaining 1/2 cup of
olive oil through the feed tube of the lid of the blender.
Let cool before using, and store refrigerated in an
airtight container.

Yield: 3/4 cup

CHURRASCO

2–4 lbs of picanha (sirloin), USDA Choice or higher
Coarse salt (thick grains of rock salt are best for this but
   if you don't have some handy use a semi-fine grain like
   Kosher salt)

Grill at medium heat—set up your grill for indirect
cooking.

When grilling a picanha you have two options: grill the
entire cut whole or cut them into steaks beforehand and
placing them on skewers. Whichever method you choose
you should first score the fat cap by making criss-crossing
cuts. This is done so that the steak doesn't curl up into a
ball on you. The fat will shrink anyway and give the meat
more flavor. To begin, place the steak on a cutting surface.
Make sure the fat layer is facing up and towards you. Next,
cut into the layer of fat in a diamond pattern. Make sure
not to cut into the steak: you just want to cut into the fat,
but not all the way through.

Seasoning Your Steak: Once you have your beautiful diamond pattern cut, you may begin seasoning your steak.
Like any good quality beef, salt is all that is needed to
bring out the best natural flavors. Coarse rock salt is tradi-
tionally used as the thicker grains help create a nice crust.
Medium grain salt is fine too, but because this is a thick
cut of beef you may need to use more than you're used to.

Grilling Your Steak: Set the flame on one side of the grill
and place the meat on the other. If you're using charcoal,
just place the briquettes on one side only. For propane
grills only turn on half the burners. You want to cook a

picanha relatively slow to avoid over-cooking. The fat dripping down also creates flare-ups which is why indirect cooking is preferred. Place the steak fat side up on the grill. Leave it like that until you see the juices rising over the fat. The meat will look like it's sweating and that's when you know it's time to flip. You may need to flip once more if it's cooking too slowly and that's fine. A must-have tool for any grilling enthusiast is a meat thermometer. This is the absolute best way to tell when meat is ready and cooked to your desired temperature. For medium-rare picanha, that would be approximately 130–35 degrees. Once the meat has reached that temperature, you're ready to start serving. Cut the steak against the grain when serving.

Serve with farofa (seasoned and toasted yucca flour) and molho a campanha (hearts of palm salad, recipe follows).

MOLHO A CAMPANHA

1 14-ounce can hearts of palm, drained, halved lengthwise
   and thinly sliced
4 medium tomatoes, chopped
1/2 cup chopped red onion
1/2 small hot chile, such as jalapeño or serrano, minced
1/4 cup chopped fresh cilantro
2 tablespoons red-wine vinegar
1/4 teaspoon kosher salt

Combine hearts of palm, tomatoes, onion, hot pepper, cilantro, vinegar, and salt in a medium bowl.

CHAPTER 3

THE DINING ROOM

One of our favorite things to do is host dinner parties. We love bringing together a group of people—some new friends, some old—to share stories, ideas, laughter, and drinks, and hopefully to inspire each other. We're big believers that a few essentials can ensure you have a great dinner party: appetizers and alcohol, a delicious meal, interesting guests, soft lighting, and great music. We never stress about having enough matching place settings; the more guests the merrier, and we prefer to mix and match vintage china with newer, more modern pieces for a whimsical, interesting table. We always ask that our friends do one of three things: tell a joke, tell a story, or sing a song.

Design-wise, one of the best parts of the house are the wall-to-wall handmade accordion doors that separate the dining and living room from the outdoors. We keep them open almost all the time, and definitely during dinner parties. Even if my cooking isn't spectacular, the ambiance that only tropical nights can create definitely is.

We found this beautifully weathered turquoise-blue sideboard (opposite) in Trancoso. With the neutral colors of the walls and wood furniture, this big pop of color is the perfect focal point for the dining room. The jewel-tone plastic cutlery (above) is practical but it looks terrific with simple white plates.

Our favorite instrument is the piano, but because of the humidity in Brazil, it's difficult to keep one tuned year-round. Breaker always brings his guitar so we are able to have some live music in the house, and it's always fun to see which guests have musical talent we never knew about or who sings beautifully in Portuguese or some other language. We like to have a book of popular sheet music in the house too, just in case. As creative people ourselves, we want as much creativity around us as possible at all times, and dinner parties make that happen.

To make sure we've got great music throughout the party, we've got a record player and a great collection of vinyl for all ages (opposite). Music keeps the energy levels high during a party, so we keep the tunes rolling. We love asking guests to choose the next album; it's fun to see what people choose, and it's a great way for guests to get to know each other.

10 OF OUR FAVORITE BRAZILIAN ALBUMS

- *CHEGA DE SAUDADE*, JOÃO GILBERTO (1959)

- *COISAS*, MOACIR SANTOS (1965)

- *ELIS*, ELIS REGINA (1966)

- *QUARTETO NOVO*, QUARTETO NOVO (1967)

- *OS MUTANTES*, OS MUTANTES (1968)

- *CONSTRUÇÃO*, CHICO BUARQUE (1971)

- *ARTHUR VEROCAI*, ARTHUR VEROCAI (1972)

- *CLUBE DA ESQUINA*, LO BORGES E MILTON NASCIMENTO (1972)

- *AZIMÜTH*, AZYMUTH (1975)

- *AFRICA BRASIL*, JORGE BEN (1976)

CHAPTER 4

THE LIVING ROOM

The living room is at the center of the house. To us, a living room should be—above all else—comfortable. Long gone are the days of a formal living room that's too pretty to be able to kick up your feet and relax. We prefer cozy furniture and a coffee table that looks better with age.

We found these amazing low-slung couches at a bar near Trancoso that was closing down. We recovered the cushions in white for a beachy, laid-back vibe. They're definitely not pristine by the time our kids leave, but the removable covers and the fact that they're white make them relatively easy to maintain with a good dose of bleach. We also love the depth of the seat—they're perfect for sitting back and catching up.

MEASUREMENTS FOR THE ULTIMATE LOUNGER*

- SEAT CUSHION SHOULD BE NO MORE THAN 16 INCHES HIGH

- SEAT DEPTH SHOULD BE AT LEAST 30 INCHES

- OBVIOUSLY, THE WIDER THE SOFA/CHAIR, THE BETTER (ESPECIALLY IF YOU'RE A FAMILY OF NINE!)

*FOR OUR VACATION HOUSE, OUR SEATING TENDS TO BE LOW TO THE GROUND LIKE THE DAYBED (LEFT), BUT FOR EVERYDAY USE, THE MEASUREMENTS ABOVE ARE PERFECT!

The daybed in the nook off of the main living room is one of our favorite spots in the house. Our goal was to make it super comfortable and flexible. It's great for reading, having an afternoon cocktail in the shade, taking a nap, and it can also double as an extra bed for guests. We love that we can all pile in to watch movies, making for a great low-key night. Over the years, we've put together big binders of DVDs for the house, complete with kid-friendly movies, dramas, thrillers, comedies, and classics.

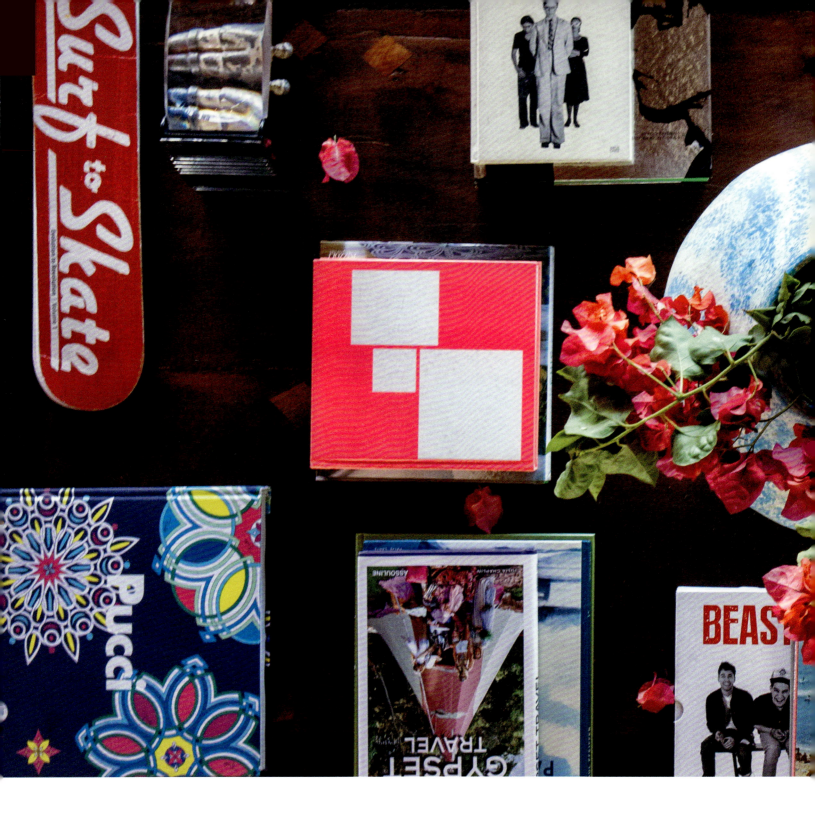

The living room is where we house our books. The coffee table and shelves have volumes devoted to design, art, fashion, music, and pop culture, as well as a great collection of novels. We ask anyone visiting us to leave a favorite book if they finish reading it while on vacation. Since our guests are from all over the world, we've ended up with an amazing array representing so many different viewpoints. If you visit and find a copy of 50 Shades of Gray, *we promise it isn't ours.*

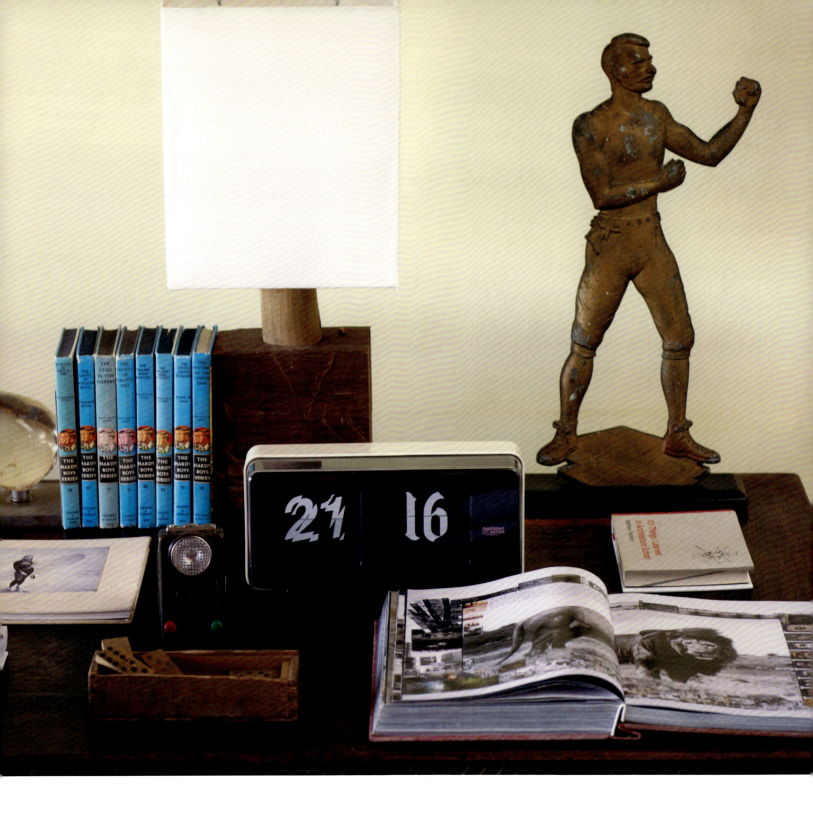

We love displaying vintage furniture and accessories we've found both in the States and in Brazil. Vintage pieces are the best way to bring a sense of warmth and character to a space, and a chance to express personality in a home. Mixing vintage pieces with modern pieces is what our design aesthetic is all about, and we feel it's the most comfortable way to live.

We're avid candle collectors: we love their soft lighting and intoxicating scents. Robert found a beautiful mummy-inspired candle that we decided to splurge on (above right). We brought it to Brazil, thinking that it would be beautiful with the natural wood in the home, but didn't imagine how quickly our next guest would choose to burn it. The mummification process proved insufficient, and the candle had withered away by the end of the guest's stay—but at least we have this picture to remind us!

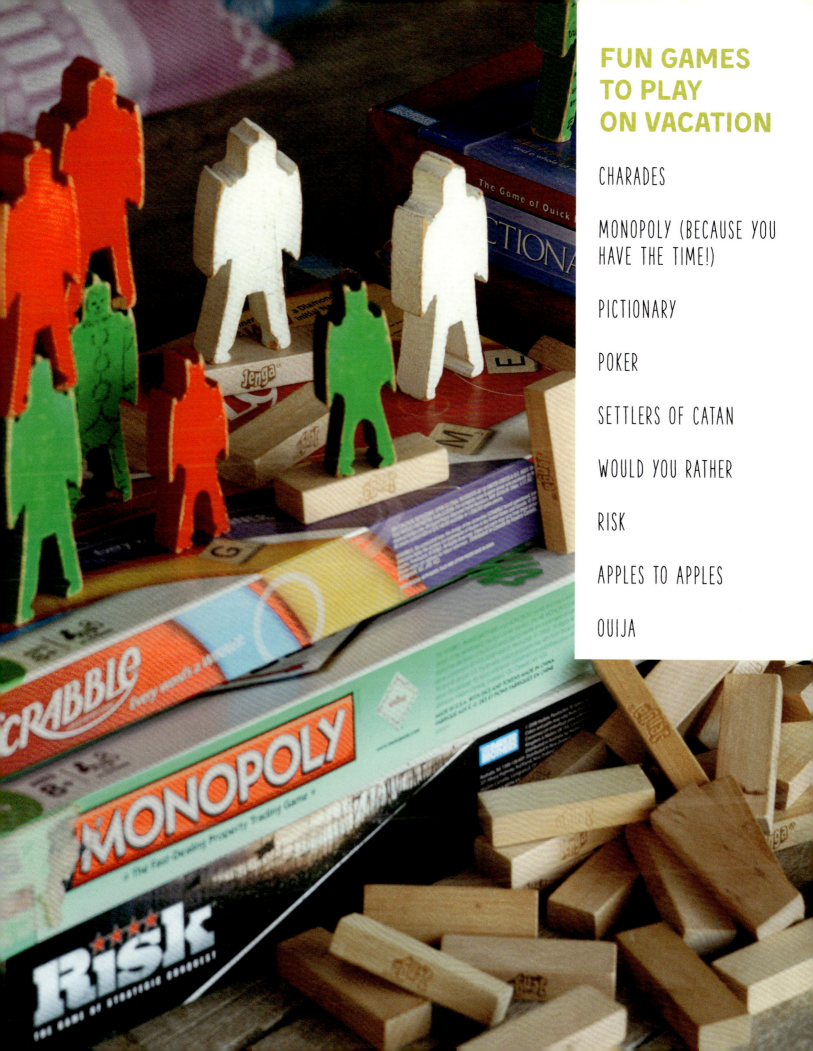

FUN GAMES TO PLAY ON VACATION

CHARADES

MONOPOLY (BECAUSE YOU HAVE THE TIME!)

PICTIONARY

POKER

SETTLERS OF CATAN

WOULD YOU RATHER

RISK

APPLES TO APPLES

OUIJA

CHAPTER 5

THE BEDROOMS

Each of the four bedrooms is in its own section of the house off of the main living and dining area. As with any great bedroom in an exotic vacation home, the bedrooms in our house are comfortable, colorful, and full of personal touches to make guests feel like they really live there. The master bedroom is no exception. Crisp, white cotton linens are perfect for the warm tropical climate, and a beautiful Missoni throw is draped at the foot of the bed for the occasional chillier nights (see pgs. 152–53). We always have a few different pillows for guests—everything from down pillows to memory foam—so every guest gets a great night's sleep. Bed posts are the perfect place to throw scarves and sarongs, and add a beautiful pop of color.

To really give guests a sense of being at home, it's important for each room to have a desk area. Whether the guest is editing photos, answering emails, or writing, a cozy space for creativity is necessary. We always have extra Moleskine notebooks and an assortment of pens and pencils in case our guests forgot theirs. Another hospitable touch is to have a pitcher of cold water next to each bed before the guests settle in for the night. We like to think we can hang with the locals all night long, but after a night of good food and our fair share of booze, nothing beats hydrating before sleep.

One of the design elements we love most in the home are the mosquito nets (opposite). Part of the beauty of the home is feeling so connected to nature. Whether you sleep with the windows open or closed, you're lulled to sleep by the steady buzz of the cicadas and awoken by the songs of the birds and sometimes even the chatter of the monkeys. That said, nothing is worse than waking up and realizing you were the late night snack for the mosquitoes. These nets are easy to find, inexpensive, and make all the difference. We have a few with beautiful embroidery that add a sweet, feminine touch.

CREATING THE PERFECT BED

- IT MAY SOUND OBVIOUS BUT CHOOSE YOUR LINENS WISELY. PARTICULARLY IN VACATION HOUSES IN WARM CLIMATES, COTTON PERCALE SHEETS ARE OFTEN THE BEST AT CREATING A COOL, CRISP BED. PERCALE IS SLIGHTLY HEAVIER THAN COTTON SATEEN BUT IT BREATHES MUCH BETTER. THREAD COUNT SHOULD BE BETWEEN 300 TO 400.

- FOR THE CRISPEST SHEETS, IRON YOUR SHEETS. STARCH IS YOUR FRIEND, WE PROMISE.

- PAY ATTENTION TO HOW YOU'RE TUCKING IN SHEETS. A HOSPITAL FOLD IS TIMELESS AND FORMAL BUT ALSO COZY. TURN YOUR TOP SHEET DOWN AT LEAST 14 INCHES OVER YOUR COVERLET TO SHOW BEAUTIFULLY EMBROIDERED DETAILS. IF YOU'RE HOSTING, LEAVE A FEW MINTS ON THE FOLDED SHEET FOR A PERSONAL TOUCH.

- BEDSPREADS AND DUVETS ARE ALWAYS BEST IN SOMEWHAT NEUTRAL PALETTES, TO ENSURE LONGEVITY. WHITES ARE OUR PERSONAL FAVORITE. FOLD YOUR SPREAD IN THIRDS IN A "Z" PATTERN SO IT'S EASY TO USE AT NIGHT.

- HAVE A FEW PILLOW OPTIONS FOR GUESTS BECAUSE EVERYONE SLEEPS DIFFERENTLY. TRY TO HAVE SEVERAL PILLOW DENSITIES ON OFFER—FIRM, MEDIUM, AND SOFT— AS WELL AS DIFFERENT FILLERS, INCLUDING DOWN, MEMORY FOAM, OR POLYFILL (FOR PEOPLE WITH ALLERGIES).

- ARRANGE YOUR PILLOWS, SHAMS, AND THROW PILLOWS HOWEVER YOU LIKE, BUT DON'T LET THEM OVERWHELM THE BED. YOUR GUEST SHOULD FEEL TIRED FROM A LONG DAY OF ADVENTURE, NOT FROM TOSSING THROW PILLOWS ONTO THE FLOOR.

The boys' room has three single beds, each with a trundle underneath, and it's one of the coziest rooms in the house. I can't tell you how many kids have slept in there; I think it was as many as twelve on one occasion. Even though we're on vacation when we're there, we try to get them to take the time to make their beds every morning. We can't say it's always successful, but we give it our best shot.

We've always been attracted to unique objects and accessories, and we want the house we live in, and those we design for clients, to be accented with them. In the boys' room, the skate decks, wicker shade lamp, miniature classical bust, and toy figurines lining the window sill hit the right note.

CHAPTER 6

THE BATHROOMS

Each room in the house has its own bathroom. The bathrooms are very simple—they're all about bringing nature in. Local artisans built the doors and countertops using the same wood found throughout the house, which gives the natural, low-key vibe we wanted. One of the best parts of the house is the outdoor shower off of the master bedroom. You feel like you're standing in the middle of the jungle showering—and in reality, you are. It's a pretty liberating feeling.

We chose saturated colors for the bathrooms, which we think are great rooms for experimentation. Choose a beautiful green or blue and your bathroom becomes an oasis. Opt for yellow or pink and you'll be invigorated every morning while you're brushing your teeth. Have fun with it—paint is affordable and easily changed.

Bathrooms are one of the easiest and most important spaces to create a hotel-like experience. Leave luxurious products for your guests—we love Kiehl's because the products are gender-neutral and have a clean scent. Beautiful hand towels give life to the space. Watch for your favorite designers' sales to stock up. Comfortable robes are also a necessity. Just be sure that the weight of the robe works with the climate. Pay attention to small details like the privacy shades on windows—we've got a line of shades with The Shade Store that we were lucky enough to try out in the Brazil house before they hit the market (opposite). It's the finishing touches like these that give a house personality and warmth.

In the tree house's bathroom, a porcelain sink sits atop an antique table that serves as the vanity. Woven baskets beneath the sink are perfect for guests to store their toiletries, so that the countertop stays clean and uncluttered. Be sure any baskets you leave for guests are made of natural materials. Nothing kills a relaxing vacation vibe like an allergic reaction to a cheap synthetic material.

*Our favorite shower, also in the tree house, is made of stones from
a local river, bringing the outside in. One of the most inventive
details in the entire house is the unique shower heads which are
fashioned from tree trunks.*

In warm climates, outdoor showers somehow feel like the
ultimate luxury, even though they are quite rustic and simple.
And when the showers are occupied, our youngest boys always
find new and inventive ways of keeping clean!

CHAPTER 7

THE TREE HOUSE

It's always been Robert's dream to build a tree house, and buying this house afforded us the perfect opportunity to finally do it. We had visited Uxua hotel, owned by Wilburt Das, and fell in love with the artistry in the details of its buildings. We hired the same artisan and architect to guide us through the process of building our own tree house. We used as many materials as we could that are native to the State of Bahia. Everything from the main posts of the tree house to the railings of the staircase were built using tree trunks and branches. We curved the staircase around an existing tree trunk for an integrated feel, and left the ceiling in the tree house exposed to show the beautiful craftsmanship of the roofing. (TIP: if you're in Trancoso and want a proper hotel experience, Uxua is the best hotel in the area—the service is impeccable. If you want to get away from your getaway, go to Divina Espelho—it's peaceful, romantic, and the owner is our wonderful friend, Helena, who happens to be the mayor. If you ever see a beautiful blonde riding a horse around town or on the beach, it's probably Helena.)

The solitude of the tree house is magical. It has a minimalist look, but still manages to feel cozy. The tree house even has its own lounge area, which separates the staircase from the rustic glass sliding doors leading to the bedroom.

We kept the colors neutral in the bedroom to complement the beautiful wood. Pops of color in flower arrangements and bedding bring life to the space. A round jute rug creates the right amount of warmth for a tropical climate, while staying within the neutral palette.

Even though being in Trancoso is all about connecting with nature and distancing ourselves from all things technological, we definitely still love our modern conveniences. But we did our best in the tree house to hide them, or at least make them blend with the decor a bit more. We built a frame for the TV from reclaimed wood and suspended it from the ceiling with thick rope (opposite). We hid a fridge, an air conditioner, and the light switches within custom wooden enclosures (above).

The closet is the best part of the tree house. Simple shelving, matching wooden hangers, and natural light make the closet the perfect dressing room. We built enough hooks for a whole week's worth of bathing suits and towels, and added beautiful baskets for organization. We're true believers that unpacking and getting suitcases out of sight is the best way to make a vacation house feel like a home. If you're renting your home, be sure to provide guests with at least two-thirds of the closet space for them to hang their belongings. Store your items elsewhere for the rental period.

CHAPTER 8

THE OUTDOORS

One of the most important factors in our decision to buy the house was that it had so much outdoor space to create nooks and special enclaves for hanging out alone or drinking late into the night with friends. The bar had great potential when we bought the house. We added art, lighting, antiques to bring in color, and great barstools to make it feel like part of the house.

Other than building the tree house, Robert's only request was that we have an amazing pizza oven (see pg. 129). We can't say we're the best at cooking the pizzas—Paula's husband John is the true expert—but we've definitely got the biggest appetites for them.

We stay cool by the pool when we're not down at the beach. We resurfaced the pool with beautiful local stones similar to the ones we used in the tree house, and refinished the deck so it has a gray, weathered look. We love the understated, natural feel the stones and the deck give the pool area.

While it may seem the pool's rock-lined surface would feel rough and jagged, it's actually an optical illusion—the stones are perfectly smooth and evenly distributed.

BAR ESSENTIALS

- CORKSCREW

- STANDARD SHAKER

- FUN GLASSWARE

- COCKTAIL NAPKINS

- LEMONS, LIMES, & OLIVES

- BAR SNACKS

- CRAFT BEERS

- CLUB SODA AND TONIC WATER

- ANGOSTURA BITTERS

- WHITE AND RED WINES, & SOMETHING BUBBLY

- LIQUOR, OF COURSE: GIN, TEQUILA, VODKA, RUM, BOURBON, COINTREAU, & VERMOUTH

The outdoor bar, pizza oven, and covered seating area are
conveniently situated next to the pool so you don't need to go
inside the house for a drink or snack.

One of our favorite nooks is under the tree house. It's so secluded from the rest of the house, and it's the perfect space to get away from the hot sun when you need a breather. It's also become a great spot for teenagers to feel like they have their own late-night spot—so important as kids get older. We'll be honest, we'd rather not know everything they're talking about, so we're happy they have this little getaway.

A beautiful chess set and comfortable spots to lounge and read round out the private nooks that every vacation home needs. If you're trying to rent out your home through one of the many rental websites, be sure to include photos of these relaxing spots— your guests will envision themselves in that moment and there will be no question about whether to book a stay.

BUILDING THE PERFECT PING PONG TABLE

- DIMENSIONS: IT SHOULD BE 9 FEET LONG BY 5 FEET WIDE, AND 2 FEET, 6 INCHES TALL

- NET HEIGHT: 6 INCHES, WITH AN OVERHANG OF 6 INCHES ON EITHER SIDE

- PAINT THE TABLE IN BRIGHT COLORS FOR THE BEST PHOTO OPS!

A pool table (previous page) and a ping pong table (left) round out the outdoor games and keep our kids entertained (when we're lucky). Our advice is to always have at least two sets of balls for the pool table, and if kids in their early twenties are staying at your house, anticipate an impromptu beer pong game.

Our kids are American so we can't say they had much of an interest in soccer before we bought the house in Brazil. But we knew they would love it once they started playing, so we put a goal in the yard. Soccer games are now one of their favorite parts of visiting Trancoso, and a new friend joins every soccer game. It's been a great way for the kids to become friends with our neighbors and other locals.

ART, TEXTILES, LIGHTING

While we always bring our own American perspective to the houses we design, it's really important that our house in Trancoso reflects the town and the culture around it. We look to other cultures to be inspired and to grow as creative people. And Trancoso and the surrounding area have provided copious amounts of inspiration. The vibrant colors, brilliant patterns, and the unabashed pairing of contrasting hues and styles, make Trancoso's shops a feast for the eyes.

Something we've noticed about America in particular is that so many people like decorating with very monochromatic, subdued color palettes: grays, whites, creams. We've never subscribed to the idea that a home has to be monochromatic to have a getaway feel, and interior design throughout Bahia is such a testament to that.

ART

For a space to be full of character and personality, it needs great art. Robert has always been so wise in collecting art that's increased in value over time, looked great in so many environments, and that speaks to who we are as a couple and a family. We've made an effort to decorate our home in Trancoso with some of our favorite pieces.

When decorating a vacation house, it's important to consider a few things. First, is the art giving off the vibe you want the home to have? If it feels stuffy or out of place, it probably is—so go with your gut and try something else. Second, are you protecting it against nature's elements properly? In Trancoso, where humidity is a major concern, we have to frame everything. Third, and most importantly, try to support the artists in your life. Whether it's a local artist (and there are many in Trancoso), or a friend from home, supporting artists in your community is one of the best ways to give back. And you can do this on a small scale, too, like when our son Wolfie asked one of his artistically inclined classmates to paint a picture to give Robert for his most recent birthday. It was such a simple gesture, but everyone was really overjoyed.

It goes without saying that that you shouldn't have anything in your vacation house that you rent out that's too expensive relative to the value of the other decor or furnishings. You have to accept that at least some of your property will be damaged if you rent your home, and you don't want to put yourself in an uncomfortable position financially. If you need to freshen things up, go to your local flea markets. They're a great place to find inexpensive, festive art that won't break the bank. We also recommend keeping an inventory of your art and checking your pieces before and after guests leave. Other than ensuring your art has been accounted for, this is also a way to keep tabs on how your art is holding up.

One of our good friends artist Anne Carrington asked to stay at our home during Carnival one year. We normally let friends stay any time in exchange for hearing their vacation stories afterwards, but Carnival is an exception. Carnival is a festive celebration which takes place immediately before Lent, the forty-day period before Easter. Carnival is peak rental season in Trancoso, so we wanted to reach some sort of agreement with Anne. It ended up being a no-brainer—she brought us an incredible work of art in exchange for her stay. We commend her efforts and ultimate success in carrying on a 9 foot tall piece of art onto a plane. We got the piece framed in Trancoso, and it's one of our favorites (see pgs. 146–47).

In addition to paintings, photographs, and unique pieces like Anne's, limited edition prints are a great way of investing in art that's not too expensive but that still has value. We recommend using websites like Exhibition A, Artspace.com, Artnet.com, and Paddle 8 to hunt for the perfect print.

TEXTILES

Trancoso's shops are filled with a limitless array of hand-dyed scarves, locally sewn lace, and vibrant blankets. While its definitely warm and humid during the summer months, scarves are a staple of women's fashion year-round. Locals don't scrimp when it comes to quality. Keep your eye out for sarongs—not only can you use them as cover-ups, but they're also great as a less bulky alternative to a towel for your beach bag. The best part about shopping for textiles in Trancoso is that you won't see any chain retail stores, so you can be certain that anything you buy will be one of a kind.

We like to leave beautiful scarves and blankets for guests to enjoy when they visit. Our motto is "put on, take off, but please don't take home."

Like most traditional textiles from other countries in South America, the textiles made in Trancoso are exquisitely colored. In one of the bedrooms, we created a layered yet simple look by combining local textiles, J Crew sarongs, classic Missoni blankets, and a throw pillow.

LIGHTING

Yet another thing people make by hand in Trancoso is beautiful lighting. Lighting is so critical to give a space the right vibe. We love playful lighting, and there's no shortage of options in Trancoso. We chose hand-woven basket weave orb pendants to light the outdoor areas for a casual feel (left), and they only look better with age. For the sprawling porch (following page), we wanted something a little more colorful—we envisioned patterned fabric drum pendants. Paula and I shopped for the perfect fabric and she took me to her local seamstress and friend, who had the confidence to make lights for the first time based off of my sketch. I was so impressed by her fearlessness and with the end results.

With a backdrop as beautiful as Trancoso, we like the fixtures and furnishings to blend in with nature. Nature speaks for itself—add textures and shapes that mimic the surrounding outdoors.

We've always been big fans of Pluma lighting (opposite)— we've used their fixtures in so many homes and for so many projects. We lugged a few to Brazil to soften the interior in the living room. The white really pops against the dark, rich woodwork, and the feathers give a hint of loftiness that we so love.

The beauty of travel is that you see things you've never seen before, like these fantastic tree-hung lights in the Quadrado (above). For outdoor lighting, we often string party lights from the trees like this to create a warm and relaxed vibe.

TRAN

CHAPTER 10

LIVING THAT BEACH LIFE

We've been lucky enough to travel to unique places, but there's no other place in the world like the Quadrado of Trancoso. Think of every retail store you can—you won't find any of them in the Quadrado. The world has become increasingly homogenous, and Trancoso has held out in the best way. It's every bit as stylish as cities like Paris and London, without an ounce of pretention.

The Quadrado is the center of town life in Trancoso. It's a town square built around a grassy field where kids and adults alike play soccer for hours on end. Restaurants and shops line the field, and at the very end stands Brazil's second oldest church, Igreja de São João Batista (following page). The stark white church, built in 1586 by Portuguese settlers, is beautiful in contrast to the bright hues of the surrounding shops and restaurants, each built of mud and clay with palm frond roofs in compliance with local laws. The best time to be in the Quadrado is at dusk.

By day, the Quadrado is fairly quiet—only a few locals and tourists meander through the square, to be met by the occasional wild horse or bevy of supermodels. At night, the atmosphere completely changes. Stores and restaurants open for business at around 4pm and don't close until midnight. Women dress in their most comfortable sundresses, and men in their linens. People trickle in and out, eating, drinking, and mingling well into the late night hours. The tropical humidity and live acoustic music set the laid-back, beachy vibe that keeps everyone happy and coming back for more (see a detailed list of our favorite shops, restaurants and hotels on pg. 200).

There are no cars allowed in the Quadrado. Cars can drive close to it on old cobblestone roads, but they must park around its perimeters. As a result, people walk, ride bikes, and ride their horses to get around town. And one of the focal points as you do stroll the Quadrado is the striking Igreja de São João Batista (opposite).

166

MARKETS

It's the simple things in life that matter most. In Trancoso, everything is sea to table. The markets have everything you need, and nothing more, which is refreshing in an era of so many choices you can feel overwhelmed. All the essentials are there for a great meal: bread, cheese, vegetables, fruit, seafood, meat, and wine.

SHOPS

Whatever your travel budget, the Quadrado has the perfect souvenirs from low-end to high-end, and they can all be easily tucked into a suitcase (unlike the souvenirs from many of our European forays). In general, truly unique design is harder and harder to find, but visiting the Quadrado is a breath of fresh air. The unassuming boutiques sell everything from clothing and accessories to handmade furniture and home goods. The indigenous crafts are known for their bright colors, embroidery, and intricate beading. The Jesuit influence is evident in the art—beautiful hand-carved and painted statues of the Virgin Mary are in many of the Quadrado's shops. It's evident how much the locals honor and appreciate nature—so many items are crafted from natural materials. Bowls and utensils are made from coconuts, and baskets are finely woven with dried palm tree leaves. The craftsmanship is impeccable. Just as each shop's exterior is painted its own color, each shop also has a wonderfully different aesthetic.

RESTAURANTS

The dining in the Quadrado is truly impressive for such a small town. What's great is that the restaurants are open year-round, not just during high season. Don't miss the ceviche and sunset at El Gordo—mouth-watering and awe-inspiring, respectively. During the high season, we have big dinners with family and friends amongst fashionistas and supermodels, and the view of the fireworks on the beach is spectacular. We've been going to El Gordo for years, and we're not sure they know our names, but they definitely know us as "the Americans."

Restaurants in Trancoso and the surrounding area range from rustic (opposite) to more luxurious (above).

NATURE

Going to Trancoso is not only about embracing a slower way of life; it's also about stepping into nature. You never know what you're going to find when you're off the beaten path. (Case in point: the monkeylike creature below—if anyone can tell us what this is, they get a prize.) As you explore, you'll see everything from inlets with boats from another time to sloths ready to cuddle (Kristen Bell, we're looking at you). The ocean is so warm it almost feels like bath water.

Not far from our house, there are incredible mud baths (following pages). It's so much better than going to a spa: the whole family can go, the kids can be as loud as they want, and it's free. The boys scale the mountains and we stay until all of our skin is as soft as a baby's.

BEACH

This image (right) was not created in Photoshop. Its colors were not saturated to give the blue sky it's amazing hue. This is a photo taken on a normal day at the beaches of Trancoso. The sun turns the earth's clay an amazing shade of orange and picks up flecks of gold in the sand. What's even more amazing is how secluded and empty so many of the beaches are. Even the horses on Trancoso's beaches are special and authentic—these aren't the old, trained horses you'll see on your cruise to Mexico; these are beautiful, almost wild horses ready to gallop at full speed. Trancoso's beaches are a magical place.

As fancy as some of the restaurants in the Quadrado are, we secretly love the beach food most. Robert's mom always used to say after a nice meal, "Well that was delicious, but give me a New York slice!" We're definitely on the same page as Robert's mom, particularly when it comes to the beach food here—and our kids are, too. The cheese grilled over an open flame and sprinkled with oregano makes the best cheese stick any of us have ever had.

BEACH CLUBS

A fabulous aspect of Trancoso's beaches is that you can either get away to the secluded beaches, or you can surround yourself with local life at the beach clubs. You can really make your vacation what you want it to be. Sundays are the busiest days at the beach clubs: people have worked and gone to school all week, and everyone is relaxing before the week begins again. All day, everyone eats, drinks, plays in the water, and walks along the beach. The people-watching is the absolute best. Families and friends tell stories and laugh all day, and no one is checking their emails.

ATHLETICS

A vacation isn't complete without activities, and Trancoso has a lot to offer. There are so many ways to stay active here that there's no need to worry about the calories you've been consuming from all the caipirinhas (drink up, baby!). Perhaps the most incredible way to be active is by practicing Brazil's martial art, capoeira, which combines elements of dance, acrobatics, and music. Our son Breaker has taken a real liking to capoeira, and he's picked it up quickly (following pages).

One of the best parts about being on holiday is that you can be whoever you want to be, almost like on Halloween. The clay tennis courts in Trancoso are beautiful enough to make anyone feel like a pro. Our son Five loves tennis, and gets a lot of inspiration from the outfits. Richie from the Royal Tenenbaums, anyone?

The Novogratzes aren't great at surfing, but the waves are small enough here that beginners can feel comfortable giving it a try. We are pretty bad at golf too, but the courses are so beautiful in Trancoso that none of us even care. The coaches are also so friendly that whether you hit a hole-in-one or hit one off the green, you're bound to have a great day of golfing.

SOCCER

All day long, adults and children alike play soccer (*futebol* in Portuguese, or football), in the grassy field of the Quadrado. You're welcome to join in at any time, but be sure to bring your A-game. There is a local saying that the ball is born on a Brazilian's foot. Some important facts about soccer in Brazil everyone should know: 1) the country has won five FIFA World Cup championships: 1958, 1962, 1970, 1994, and 2002; 2) Brazil is home to the best female soccer player of all time, simply known as Marta (Pelé has called her "Pelé with skirts"); and 3) Brazil's arch-rival is Argentina, so don't wear Argentina's colors—white and blue—in Brazil, especially at a soccer match.

AROUND TOWN

When we first visited Trancoso, felt the bumpy roads, and noticed how slowly we were forced to drive, we were frustrated to be honest. It took some time for us to grow accustomed to the pace, but now that we have, we recognize how nice it is. In addition to the dune buggy which is one of our favorite ways to get around town (see pg. 206), the all terrain vehicle (or ATV) is another fun mode of transportation. We love riding it, and so do our kids. We've taught the oldest ones to drive on the dirt roads, so they can't cause too much damage. And because everyone drives slowly, they've learned to as well which offers some peace of mind.

ITAPORANGA VILLAGE

The Indian village of Itaporanga has been one of the most influential parts of Trancoso for our family. The locals grow up with forest animals as pets—birds, sloths, turtles, and many others are domesticated too. The village's aesthetic has had such a lasting effect. Our kids had their faces painted one year, and we loved the angular lines and colors so much that it inspired us to make our Geo Arrow fabric we've created for The Shade Store. More than anything, watching the locals perform their rituals reminds us of how important it is to be still and give thanks.

HOLIDAYS

All holidays are special in Trancoso, but Carnival is the most wonderful one of them all (*Carnaval do Brasil* in Portuguese). It's a festival celebrated in Brazil similar to Louisiana's Mardi Gras, and held between Ash Wednesday and Good Friday, marking the beginning of Lent, the forty-day period before Easter. It's the most famous holiday in Brazil—Carnival draws over 4 million people every year to its cities and towns. Rio de Janeiro hosts the biggest, most well-known party, but Trancoso's party is also sizeable. The town swells from 5,000 to 50,000 people during Carnival.

Don't get us wrong, we love hanging out with our kids—but there's another world out there, and Carnival is a great reminder of that. Everyone deserves the experience of partying all night in a foreign country to live music and watching fireworks and the sunrise on the beach. If you're lucky enough to be in Trancoso for New Year's Day, which is also a big holiday, be sure to bring an all-white outfit and some breath mints in case you fall in love.

EASTER

Robert was raised Catholic, and I was raised Baptist. We won't go into religion—that's a different book—but we will say that we love going to church once a week for solitude and reflection. And we really love that all of our seven kids have to be quiet for an hour.

Decorating Easter eggs is the best in Trancoso—the dye is so saturated, and there are so many creative local friends and neighbors who love to dye the eggs with us. It's also stress-free because all of the surfaces in our house are so easy to clean; our kitchen table is made of distressed wood, and our floors are concrete. Not worrying about spills makes the whole process so much more enjoyable.

PLACES TO STAY, EAT, AND SHOP

LODGING

Casa De Novogratz (of course!)
www.casadenovogratz.com

Uxua Casa Hotel & Spa
Quadrado
Trancoso, Brazil
Tel: +55 (73) 3668-2277
uxua.com

Divino Espelho
Estrada Trancoso Caraíva,
Km 21, s/n
Praia do Espelho
Porto Seguro, Brazil
Tel: +55 (73) 3668-1380
www.divinoespelho.com.br

Club Med
KM 18 Fazenda Taipe
Trancoso, Brazil
Tel: +55 (73) 3575-8400
clubmed.com/br

RESTAURANTS

Estrela d'Agua on Praia
dos Nativos
Estrada Arraial D'Ajuda
Trancoso, Brazil
Tel: + 55 (73) 3668-1030
Email: reservas@
estreladagua.com.br
www.estreladagua.com.br

Barraca do Jonas
Praia dos Coqueiros
Trancoso, Brazil
Tel: +55 (73) 3668-1160

El Gordo
Praça São João, 7
Trancoso, Brazil
Tel: +55 (73) 3668-1193
www.elgordotrancoso.com.br

Maritaca
Rua do Telégrafo, 388
Trancoso, Brazil
Tel: +55 (73) 3668-1702

Portinha
Rua do Mucugê, 333
Arraial D'Ajuda, Bahia
Tel: +55 (73) 3575-1882
Email: contato@portinha.com.br
www.portinha.com.br

Silvinha
Praia do Espelho
Trancoso, Brazil
Tel: +55 (73) 9985-4157

Capim Santo
Rua do Beco, 55
Trancoso, Brazil
Tel: +55 (73) 3668-1122
www.capimsanto.com.br

Cacau
Praça São João 96
Trancoso, Brazil
Tel: +55 (73) 3668-1266
ocacautrancoso.com.br

SHOPPING

Inn Brazil
Quadrado
Trancoso, Brazil
Tel: +55 (73) 3668-1259
Email: pedroalves56@
yahoo.co.uk
inn-brazil.com

MTrancoso
Tel: +55 (11) 3816-1298
mtrancoso.com

Danielle Rothmann
Quadrado
Trancoso, Brazil
daniellerothmann.com

Osklen
Praça São João, 5, Quadrado
Trancoso, Brazil
Tel: +55 73 3668 1090
osklen.com

Mucugê Street (a street in
a nearby town filled with
shops and restaurants)
Arraial d'Ajuda, Brazil

A FEW KEY PHRASES IN PORTUGUESE

Part of what's amazing about going to another place is immersing yourself in the culture. When we visit Trancoso, we usually go around Easter when the kids are out of school for spring break. The kids love visiting the local school to learn more about the kids their age and to try to pick up more Portuguese. Here are a few basic words and phrases you'll want to know if you visit:

PORTUGESE	ENGLISH
OI!	HI!
BOM DIA	GOOD MORNING
BOA TARDE	GOOD AFTERNOON
BOA NOITE	GOOD EVENING / GOODNIGHT
COMO VAI?	HOW ARE YOU?
TUDO BOM!	GREAT!
OBRIGADA / OBRIGADO	THANK YOU [FOR WOMEN] / THANK YOU [FOR MEN]
TCHAU!	BYE!
ME DIVERTI MUITO!	I HAD A LOT OF FUN!
POR FAVOR	PLEASE
DESCULPE!	I'M SORRY! / EXCUSE ME!
DESCULPE, NÃO ENTENDI	SORRY, I DIDN'T UNDERSTAND
COMO É SUE NOME?	WHAT'S YOUR NAME?
MEU NOME É _____	MY NAME IS _____
SOU DE _____	I AM FROM _____
MUITO PRAZER	NICE TO MEET YOU
IGUALMENTE	LIKEWISE
QUANTO FOO A CONGA?	HOW MUCH WAS THE BILL? [ASKING FOR A BILL AT A RESTAURANT]
CERVEJA	BEER
CACHAÇA	SUGAR CANE RUM (MOST POPULAR BRAZILIAN LIQUOR)
O QUE SIGNIFIER _____?	WHAT DOES _____ MEAN?
COMO?	WHAT?
SIM	YES
NÃO	NO

ABOUT THE AUTHORS

Robert and Cortney Novogratz met at a party twenty years ago and have been together ever since. Native Southerners, and both from large families, the couple moved to New York to pursue a job on Wall Street (Robert) and acting (Cortney). After realizing they had a knack for renovating derelict properties into coveted, gorgeously designed homes, they put their talents to use full-time and founded The Novogratz, their eponymous design firm. They have designed and developed many unique properties in cities around the country, from New York City to Napa Valley. They recently moved to Los Angeles with their seven children and renovated a 1920s house in the Hollywood Hills, known as the Castle.

COPYRIGHT

First published in the United States in 2016 by
Rizzoli International Publications, Inc.
300 Park Avenue South
New York, NY 10010
www.rizzoliusa.com

2016 2017 2018 / 10 9 8 7 6 5 4 3 2 1

ISBN: 978-0-8478-4808-9
Library of Congress Control Number: 2016742715

Printed in China

Designed by Kayleigh Jankowski

PHOTO CREDITS

Guy Aroch: 139; Ariadna Bufi: 2, 3, 4, 5, 9, 14, 16–17, 22, 24, 27, 28, 38–39, 62–63, 64, 65, 66, 72–73, 81 top, 82, 84, 85, 87 left, 87 top right, 94, 103, 105, 106, 110–11, 116, 117 top left, 117 right, 120, 124, 126–27, 129, 134–35, 140, 142, 146, 148, 155, 156, 161, 164, 170, 172, 174, 175, 187; Roberto D'Addona: 8, 60, 70, 168, 178; Ale Gabeira: 11, 13, 97, 112, 115, 119 right, 125; Tim Geaney: 6–7, 30, 51, 83, 87 bottom right, 93 top right, 104, 108, 113, 114, 117 bottom left, 118, 119 top left, 119 bottom left, 131, 136, 154, 166, 169, 171, 176 top left, 182, 184, 186, 188; Catherine Hall: 15, 32, 40–41, 43, 50, 53, 68, 69, 74–75, 78–79, 80, 96, 107, 132, 133, 153, 167, 180, 181, 183, 185, 189, 190, 192, 198, 204–05; Bethany Nauert: 31, 33, 42, 52, 81 bottom left, 150; Costas Picadas: 36, 46, 88, 98–99, 138, 202–03, 206; Lucas Raymond: 48–49, 67, 81 bottom right, 93 left, 93 bottom right, 100–101, 139 left, 173, 176 bottom left, 177, 179, 193, 194, 195; Denis Sytman: 199; Matthew Williams: 76, 91, 92, 122, 128, 130, 145, 147, 149, 158, 159, 160

THIS BOOK IS DEDICATED TO PAULA

*Our love for Paula is as strong as our love for Brazil.
She is everything—a sister, a mother, a friend, a teacher—
not only to our family but also to guests from around
the world. Every time we read a new guest book entry or
get an email about someone's trip to the house, they rave
about Paula as much as they rave about Trancoso.
Paula, you are the hostess with the mostess.*